How Do I Love Thee?

How Do I Love Thee?

Beautiful Love Poems of Yesterday and Today

Selected by Benjamin Whitley

With Photographic Illustrations

♛ Hallmark Crown Editions

"Men Marry What They Need. I Marry You." by John Ciardi. © Rutgers, The State University 1958. Reprinted by permission of the author. "My Delight and Thy Delight" by Robert Bridges from The Poetical Works of Robert Bridges. *By permission of The Clarendon Press, Oxford. "It May Not Always Be So" by E. E. Cummings. Copyright, 1923, 1951 by E. E. Cummings. Reprinted from his volume* Poems 1923-1954 *by permission of Harcourt Brace Jovanovich, Inc. "My Love Comes Walking" by Mark Van Doren. Reprinted by permission of Hill and Wang, A division of Farrar, Straus & Giroux, from* Collected and New Poems 1924-1963 *by Mark Van Doren. Copyright © 1963 by Mark Van Doren. "Oh, When I Was in Love" by A. E. Housman. From "A Shropshire Lad"—Authorised Edition—from* The Collected Poems of A. E. Housman. *Copyright 1939, 1940, © 1965 by Holt, Rinehart and Winston, Inc. Copyright © 1967, 1968 by Robert E. Symons. Reprinted by permission of Holt, Rinehart and Winston, Inc., The Society of Authors as the literary representative of the Estate of A. E. Housman and Jonathan Cape Ltd., publishers of A. E. Housman's* Collected Poems. *"Intoxication" by Boris Pasternak from* Poems of Doctor Zhivago. *Reprinted by permission of the translator, Eugene M. Kayden. "Spring Night" reprinted with permission of The Macmillan Company from* Collected Poems *by Sara Teasdale. Copyright 1915 by The Macmillan Company, renewed 1943 by Mamie T. Wheless. "Love-Song" by Rainer Maria Rilke,* Selected Works, II, *translated by J. B. Leishman. © The Hogarth Press Ltd. 1960. Reprinted by permission of New Directions Publishing Corporation, St. John's College, Oxford and The Hogarth Press Ltd. "For Miriam" by Kenneth Patchen,* Collected Poems. *Copyright 1942 by New Directions Publishing Corporation. Reprinted by permission of New Directions Publishing Corporation. "An Immorality" by Ezra Pound,* Lustra. *Copyright 1917 by Ezra Pound. Reprinted by permission of New Directions Publishing Corporation, agent for the Committee for Ezra Pound. "Love Song" by William Carlos Williams,* Collected Earlier Poems. *Copyright 1938 by William Carlos Williams. Reprinted by permission of New Directions Publishing Corporation. "Poem In Prose" by Archibald MacLeish. Copyright 1948 by Archibald MacLeish. Reprinted from* Actfive and Other Poems, *by Archibald MacLeish, by permission of Random House, Inc. "Love Song" by Elinor Wylie. Copyright 1929 by Alfred A. Knopf, Inc., and renewed 1957 by Edwina C. Rubenstein. Reprinted from* Collected Poems of Elinor Wylie, *by permission of Alfred A. Knopf, Inc. "Love Is" (Copyright 1949 May Swenson) is reprinted by permission of Charles Scribner's Sons from* To Mix With Time *by May Swenson. "Rain" by Jean Starr Untermeyer. Reprinted by permission of Michel B. Farano, Literary Executor for Jean Starr Untermeyer.*

PHOTOGRAPHIC CREDITS
*Art Expo—page 48
Jim Cozad/Harv Gariety—6
Colour Library—64
Phoebe Dunn—18
Richard Fanolio—front endpaper, 14, 54
Harv Gariety—10, 38, 42, 56, back endpaper
Carol Hale—36
Carter Hamilton—30
Rod Hanna—24
Maxine Jacobs—22
Jim Lipp—45
Walter W. Plessner—12
H. Armstrong Roberts—61
Walter Shostal—52
Ed Simpson—5, 40
Otto Storch—28, 32
Sam Zarember—title page*

The Poems

HOW DO I LOVE THEE?

How do I love thee? Let me count the ways.
I love thee to the depth and breadth and height
My soul can reach, when feeling out of sight
For the ends of Being and ideal Grace.
I love thee to the level of every day's
Most quiet need, by sun and candlelight.
I love thee freely, as men strive for Right;
I love thee purely, as they turn from Praise.
I love thee with the passion put to use
In my old griefs, and with my childhood's faith.
I love thee with a love I seemed to lose
With my lost saints—I love thee with the breath,
Smiles, tears, of all my life!—and, if God choose,
I shall but love thee better after death.

— Elizabeth Barrett Browning

4

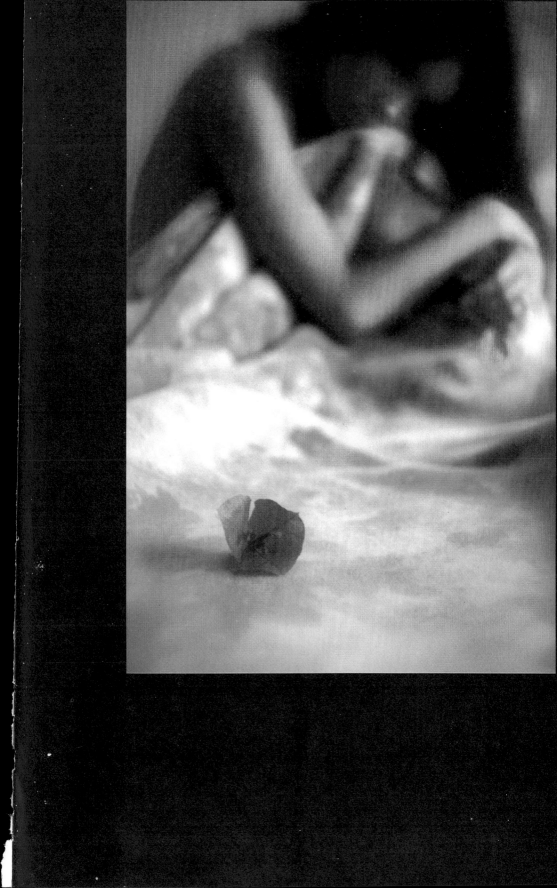

TO MY DEAR AND LOVING HUSBAND

If ever two were one, then surely we.
If ever man were lov'd by wife, then thee.
If ever wife was happy in a man,
Compare with me, ye women, if you can.
I prize thy love more than whole mines of gold,
Of all the riches that the East doth hold.
My love is such that rivers cannot quench,
Nor ought but love from thee give recompense.
Thy love is such I can no way repay;
The heavens reward thee manifold I pray.
Then while we live, in love let's so persevere,
That when we live no more, we may live ever.

— Anne Bradstreet

ANNABEL LEE

It was many and many a year ago,
  In a kingdom by the sea
That a maiden there lived whom you may know
  By the name of Annabel Lee;—
And this maiden she lived with no other thought
  Than to love and be loved by me.

I was a child and she was a child,
  In this kingdom by the sea,
But we loved with a love that was more than love—
  I and my Annabel Lee—
With a love that the winged seraphs in Heaven
  Coveted her and me.

And this was the reason that, long ago,
  In this kingdom by the sea,
A wind blew out of a cloud, chilling
  My beautiful Annabel Lee;
So that her high-born kinsmen came
  And bore her away from me,
To shut her up in a sepulcher
  In this kingdom by the sea.

The angels, not half so happy in Heaven,
  Went envying her and me:—
Yes!—that was the reason (as all men know,
  In this kingdom by the sea)
That the wind came out of the cloud, by night,
  Chilling and killing my Annabel Lee.

But our love it was stronger by far than the love
   Of those who were older than we —
   Of many far wiser than we —
And neither the angels in Heaven above,
   Nor the demons down under the sea,
Can ever dissever my soul from the soul
   Of the beautiful Annabel Lee: —

For the moon never beams without bringing me dreams
   Of the beautiful Annabel Lee;
And the stars never rise but I feel the bright eyes
   Of the beautiful Annabel Lee;
And so, all the night-tide, I lie down by the side
Of my darling, — my darling, — my life and my bride,
   In the sepulcher there by the sea —
   In her tomb by the sounding sea.

— *Edgar Allan Poe*

SONG TO CELIA

Drink to me only with thine eyes,
    And I will pledge with mine;
Or leave a kiss but in the cup,
    And I'll not look for wine.
The thirst that from the soul doth rise
    Doth ask a drink divine;
But might I of Jove's nectar sup,
    I would not change for thine.

I sent thee late a rosy wreath,
    Not so much honoring thee
As giving it a hope that there
    It could not withered be.
But thou thereon didst only breathe,
    And sent'st it back to me;
Since when it grows, and smells, I swear,
    Not of itself but thee.

—Ben Jonson

LOVERS' WINE

How dazzling are the heavens to-day!
Without bridle, bit or spurs, away!
Let's leave, on a steed of soaring wine,
For a faery realm and skies divine!

Oh like two angels tortured by
A pitiless fever let us fly
And the beckoning far mirage pursue
That glitters in morning's crystal blue!

Softly swaying on the wing
Of fancy's whirlwind we shall ride,
In a twin delirium glorying
And racing on, love, side by side;
So, tireless, truceless, we shall rise,
To reach my dreamer's paradise!

—Charles Baudelaire

SHE WALKS IN BEAUTY

She walks in beauty, like the night
*   Of cloudless climes and starry skies;*
And all that's best of dark and bright
*   Meet in her aspect and her eyes:*
Thus mellowed to that tender light
*   Which heaven to gaudy day denies.*

One shade the more, one ray the less,
*   Had half impaired the nameless grace*
Which waves in every raven tress,
*   Or softly lightens o'er her face;*
Where thoughts serenely sweet express
*   How pure, how dear, their dwelling-place.*

And on that cheek, and o'er that brow,
*   So soft, so calm, yet eloquent,*
The smiles that win, the tints that glow,
*   But tell of days in goodness spent,*
A mind at peace with all below,
*   A heart whose love is innocent!*

—George Gordon, Lord Byron

DOVER BEACH

The sea is calm to-night.
The tide is full, the moon lies fair
Upon the straits;—on the French coast the light
Gleams and is gone; the cliffs of England stand,
Glimmering and vast, out in the tranquil bay.
Come to the window, sweet is the night-air!
Only, from the long line of spray
Where the sea meets the moon-blanched land,
Listen! you hear the grating roar
Of pebbles which the waves draw back, and fling,
At their return, up the high strand,
Begin, and cease, and then again begin,
With tremulous cadence slow, and bring
The eternal note of sadness in.

Sophocles long ago
Heard it on the Aegean, and it brought
Into his mind the turbid ebb and flow
Of human misery; we
Find also in the sound a thought,
Hearing it by this distant northern sea.
The sea of faith
Was once, too, at the full, and round earth's shore
Lay like the folds of a bright girdle furled.
But now I only hear
Its melancholy, long, withdrawing roar,
Retreating, to the breath
Of the night-wind, down the vast edges drear
And naked shingles of the world.

Ah, love, let us be true
To one another! for the world, which seems
To lie before us like a land of dreams,
So various, so beautiful, so new,
Hath really neither joy, nor love, nor light,
Nor certitude, nor peace, nor help for pain;
And we are here as on a darkling plain
Swept with confused alarms of struggle and flight,
Where ignorant armies clash by night.

— Matthew Arnold

17

LOVE-SONG

How shall I hold my soul, that it may not
be touching yours? How shall I lift it then
above you to where other things are waiting?
Ah, gladly would I lodge it, all-forgot,
with some lost thing the dark is isolating
on some remote and silent spot that, when
your depths vibrate, is not itself vibrating.
You and me—all that lights upon us, though,
brings us together like a fiddle-bow
drawing one voice from two strings it glides along.
Across what instrument have we been spanned?
And what violinist holds us in his hand?
O sweetest song.

MY DELIGHT AND THY DELIGHT

My delight and thy delight
Walking, like two angels white,
In the gardens of the night:

My desire and thy desire
Twining to a tongue of fire,
Leaping live, and laughing higher:

Thro' the everlasting strife
In the mystery of life.
Love, from whom the world begun,
Hath the secret of the sun.

Love can tell, and love alone,
Whence the million stars were strewn,
Why each atom knows its own,
How, in spite of woe and death,
Gay is life, and sweet is breath:

This he taught us, this we knew,
Happy is his science true,
Hand in hand as we stood
'Neath the shadows of the wood,
Heart to heart as we lay
In the dawning of the day.

— Robert Bridges

20

INTOXICATION

Neath a willow with ivy entangled
We take cover in blustery weather.
My arms are wreathed about you;
In my raincape we huddle together.

I was wrong: Not ivy, my dearest,
But hops encircle this willow.
Well, then, let's spread in its shelter
My cape for a rug and a pillow!

— Boris Pasternak

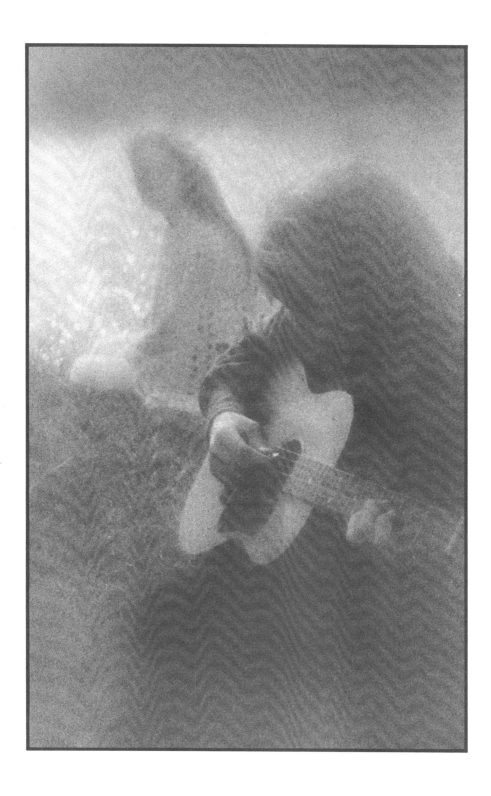

AN IMMORALITY

Sing we for love and idleness,
Naught else is worth the having.

Though I have been in many a land,
There is naught else in living.

And I would rather have my sweet,
Though rose-leaves die of grieving,

Than do high deeds in Hungary
To pass all men's believing.

— Ezra Pound

LOVE IS

a rain of diamonds
in the mind

the soul's fruit
sliced in two

a dark spring
loosed at the lips of light

under-earth waters
unlocked from their lurking
to sparkle in a crevice
parted by the sun

a temple
not of stone but cloud
beyond the heart's roar
and all violence

outside the anvil-stunned domain
unfrenzied space

between the grains of change
blue permanence

one short step
to the good ground

bite into bread again

— May Swenson

MEETING AT NIGHT

The grey sea and the long black land;
And the yellow half-moon large and low;
And the startled little waves that leap
In fiery ringlets from their sleep,
As I gain the cove with pushing prow,
And quench its speed i' the slushy sand.

Then a mile of warm, sea-scented beach;
Three fields to cross till a farm appears;
A tap at the pane, the quick sharp scratch
And blue spurt of a lighted match,
And a voice less loud, through its joys and fears,
Than the two hearts beating each to each!

— Robert Browning

A DECADE

When you came, you were like red wine and honey,
And the taste of you burnt my mouth with its sweetness.
Now you are like morning bread,
Smooth and pleasant.
I hardly taste you at all, for I know your savor;
But I am completely nourished.

— Amy Lowell

OH, WHEN I WAS IN LOVE

Oh, when I was in love with you,
　　Then I was clean and brave,
And miles around the wonder grew
　　How well I did behave.

And now the fancy passes by,
　　And nothing will remain,
And miles around they'll say that I
　　Am quite myself again.

— A. E. Housman

29

MEN MARRY WHAT THEY NEED. I MARRY YOU

Men marry what they need. I marry you,
morning by morning, day by day, night by night,
and every marriage makes this marriage new.

In the broken name of heaven, in the light
that shatters granite, by the spitting shore,
in air that leaps and wobbles like a kite,

I marry you from time and a great door
is shut and stays shut against wind, sea, stone,
sunburst, and heavenfall. And home once more

inside our walls of skin and struts of bone,
man-woman, woman-man, and each the other,
I marry you by all dark and all dawn

and learn to let time spend. Why should I bother
the flies about me? Let them buzz and do.
Men marry their queen, their daughter, or their mother

by names they prove, but that thin buzz whines through:
when reason falls to reasons, cause is true.
Men marry what they need. I marry you.

—John Ciardi

31

SHALL I COMPARE THEE TO A SUMMER'S DAY?

Shall I compare thee to a summer's day?
Thou art more lovely and more temperate.
Rough winds do shake the darling buds of May,
And summer's lease hath all too short a date:
Sometime too hot the eye of heaven shines,
And often is his gold complexion dimm'd;
And every fair from fair sometime declines,
By chance or nature's changing course untrimm'd;
But thy eternal summer shall not fade,
Nor lose possession of that fair thou owest;
Nor shall Death brag thou wander'st in his shade,
When in eternal lines to time thou grow'st.
So long as men can breathe, or eyes can see,
So long lives this, and this gives life to thee.

— William Shakespeare

JENNY KISS'D ME

Jenny kiss'd me when we met,
*   Jumping from the chair she sat in;*
Time, you thief, who love to get
*   Sweets into your list, put that in!*
Say I'm weary, say I'm sad,
*   Say that health and wealth have miss'd me,*
Say I'm growing old, but add,
*   Jenny kiss'd me.*

—Leigh Hunt

Song from AGLAURA

Why so pale and wan, fond lover?
 Prithee, why so pale?
Will, when looking well can't move her,
 Looking ill prevail?
 Prithee, why so pale?

Why so dull and mute, young sinner?
 Prithee, why so mute?
Will, when speaking well can't win her,
 Saying nothing do 't?
 Prithee, why so mute?

Quit, quit for shame! This will not move;
 This cannot take her.
If of herself she will not love,
 Nothing can make her:
 The devil take her!

— Sir John Suckling

35

THE PASSIONATE SHEPHERD TO HIS LOVE

Come live with me and be my love,
And we will all the pleasures prove
That hills and valleys, dales and fields,
Or woods or steepy mountain yields.

And we will sit upon the rocks,
And see the shepherds feed their flocks
By shallow rivers, to whose falls
Melodious birds sing madrigals.

And I will make thee beds of roses
And a thousand fragrant posies;
A cap of flowers, and a kirtle
Embroider'd all with leaves of myrtle.

A gown made of the finest wool
Which from our pretty lambs we pull;
Fair-lined slippers for the cold,
With buckles of the purest gold.

A belt of straw and ivy-buds
With coral clasps and amber studs:
And if these pleasures may thee move,
Come live with me and be my love.

—Christopher Marlowe

LOVE SONG

Sweep the house clean,
hang fresh curtains
in the windows
put on a new dress
and come with me!

The elm is scattering
its little loaves
of sweet smells
from a white sky!

Who shall hear of us
in the time to come?
Let him say there was
a burst of fragrance
from black branches.

— *William Carlos Williams*

39

THE INDIAN SERENADE

I arise from dreams of thee
In the first sweet sleep of night,
When the winds are breathing low,
And the stars are shining bright:
I arise from dreams of thee,
And a spirit in my feet
Hath led me — who knows how?
To thy chamber window, Sweet!

The wandering airs they faint
On the dark, the silent stream —
The Champak odors fail
Like sweet thoughts in a dream;
The nightingale's complaint,
It dies upon her heart; —
As I must on thine,
Oh, beloved as thou art!

Oh lift me from the grass! —
I die! I faint! I fail!
Let thy love in kisses rain
On my lips and eyelids pale.
My cheek is cold and white, alas!
My heart beats loud and fast; —
Oh! press it to thine own again,
Where it will break at last.

— Percy Bysshe Shelley

I GAVE MYSELF

I gave myself to him,
And took himself for pay.
The solemn contract of life
Was ratified this way.

The wealth might disappoint,
Myself a poorer prove
Than this great purchaser suspect,
The daily own of Love.

Depreciate the vision;
But, till the merchant buy,
Still fable, in the isles of spice,
The subtle cargoes lie.

At least, 'tis mutual risk,—
Some found it mutual gain;
Sweet debt of Life,—each night to owe,
Insolvent, every noon.

— Emily Dickinson

43

POEM IN PROSE

This poem is for my wife
I have made it plainly and honestly
The mark is on it
Like the burl on the knife

I have not made it for praise
She has no more need for praise
Than summer has
On the bright days

In all that becomes a woman
Her words and her ways are beautiful
Love's lovely duty
The well-swept room

Wherever she is there is sun
And time and a sweet air
Peace is there
Work done

There are always curtains and flowers
And candles and baked bread
And a cloth spread
And a clean house

Her voice when she sings is a voice
At dawn by a freshening sea
Where the wave leaps in the
Wind and rejoices

Wherever she is it is now
It is here where the apples are
Here in the stars
In the quick hour

The greatest and richest good—
My own life to live—
This she has given me

If giver could

— Archibald MacLeish

44

SONNETS—UNREALITIES
I

it may not always be so; and i say
that if your lips, which i have loved, should touch
another's, and your dear strong fingers clutch
his heart, as mine in time not far away;
if on another's face your sweet hair lay
in such a silence as i know, or such
great writhing words as, uttering overmuch,
stand helplessly before the spirit at bay;

if this should be, i say if this should be—
you of my heart, send me a little word;
that i may go unto him, and take his hands,
saying, Accept all happiness from me.
then shall i turn my face, and hear one bird
sing terribly afar in the lost lands.

—e. e. cummings

THE GARDEN OF LOVE

I went to the Garden of Love
And saw what I never had seen:
A Chapel was built in the midst,
Where I used to play on the green.

And the gates of this Chapel were shut,
And "Thou shalt not" writ over the door;
So I turned to the Garden of Love
That so many sweet flowers bore;

And I saw it was filled with graves,
And tombstones where flowers should be;
And priests in black gowns were walking their rounds,
And binding with briars my joys and desires.

— William Blake

A RED, RED ROSE

O, my luve is like a red, red rose,
That's newly sprung in June:
O, my luve is like the melodie
That's sweetly played in tune.

As fair art thou, my bonnie lass,
So deep in luve am I;
And I will luve thee still, my dear,
Till a' the seas gang dry.

Till a' the seas gang dry, my dear,
And the rocks melt wi' the sun;
And I will luve thee still, my dear,
While the sands o' life shall run.

And fare thee well, my only luve!
And fare thee well awhile!
And I will come again, my luve,
Tho' it were ten thousand mile!

— Robert Burns

LOVE SONG

Had I concealed my love
And you so loved me longer,
Since all the wise reprove
Confession of that hunger
In any human creature,
It had not been my nature.

I could not so insult
The beauty of that spirit
Who like a thunderbolt
Has broken me, or near it;
To love I have been candid,
Honest, and open-handed.

Although I love you well
And shall for ever love you,
I set that archangel
The depths of heaven above you;
And I shall lose you, keeping
His word, and no more weeping.

— Elinor Wylie

MY FAMILIAR DREAM

I often dream strange penetrating dreams
Of one whom I adore and who loves me,
Whose image changes yet unchanging seems,
Who loves me well and understandingly.
No darkness is there in my heart for her:
For her alone its secrets all are plain:
She cools my pale, moist forehead, while her prayer
Restores me, and her tears console my pain.
And is she fair or dark? I do not know.
Her name: 'Tis musical, recalling those
Of loved ones whom Life exiled long ago.
Her gaze is like a statue's, and her voice
—Her voice is grave and calm and is withdrawn,
Like those of dear ones gone beyond the bourne.

— Paul Verlaine

BELIEVE ME,
IF ALL THOSE ENDEARING YOUNG CHARMS

Believe me, if all those endearing young charms,
Which I gaze on so fondly to-day,
Were to change by to-morrow, and fleet in my arms,
Like fairy-gifts fading away,
Thou wouldst still be adored, as this moment thou art,
Let thy loveliness fade as it will,
And around the dear ruin each wish of my heart
Would entwine itself verdantly still.

It is not while beauty and youth are thine own,
And thy cheeks unprofaned by a tear,
That the fervor and faith of a soul may be known,
To which time will but make thee more dear!
No, the heart that has truly loved never forgets,
But as truly loves on to the close,
As the sunflower turns to her god when he sets
The same look which she turned when he rose!

— *Thomas Moore*

MY LOVE COMES WALKING

My love comes walking,
And these flowers
That never saw her til this day
Look up; but then
Bend down straightway.

My love sees nothing here but me,
Who never trembled thus before;
And glances down
Lest I do more.

My love is laughing;
Those wild things
Were never tame until I too,
Down-dropping, kissed
Her silvery shoe.

— Mark Van Doren

FOR MIRIAM

Do I not deal with angels
When her lips I touch

So gentle, so warm and sweet — falsity
Has no sight of her
O the world is a place of veils and roses
When she is there

I am come to her wonder
Like a boy finding a star in a haymow
And there is nothing cruel or mad or evil
Anywhere

— Kenneth Patchen

I WISH I COULD REMEMBER THAT FIRST DAY

I wish I could remember that first day,
First hour, first moment of your meeting me,
If bright or dim the season, it might be
Summer or winter for aught I can say;
So unrecorded did it slip away,
So blind was I to see and to foresee,
So dull to mark the budding of my tree
That would not blossom yet for many a May.
If only I could recollect it, such
A day of days! I let it come and go
As traceless as a thaw of bygone snow;
It seemed to mean so little, meant so much;
If only now I could recall that touch,
First touch of hand in hand—did one but know!

—Christina Rossetti

RAIN

I have always hated the rain,
And the gloom of grayed skies.
But now I think I must always cherish
Rain-hung leaf and the misty river;
And the friendly screen of dripping green
Where eager kisses were shyly given
And your pipe-smoke made clouds
   in our damp, close heaven.

The curious laggard passed us by,
His wet shoes soughed on the shining walk.
And that afternoon was filled with a blurred glory—
That afternoon, when we first talked as lovers.

—Jean Starr Untermeyer

SPRING NIGHT

The park is filled with night and fog,
The veils are drawn about the world,
The drowsy lights along the paths
Are dim and pearled.

Gold and gleaming the empty streets,
Gold and gleaming the misty lake,
The mirrored lights like sunken swords,
Glimmer and shake.

Oh, is it not enough to be
Here with this beauty over me?
My throat should ache with praise, and I
Should kneel in joy beneath the sky.
O, beauty are you not enough?
Why am I crying after love,
With youth, a singing voice and eyes
To take earth's wonder with surprise?
Why have I put off my pride,
Why am I unsatisfied, —
I for whom the pensive night
Binds her cloudy hair with light, —
I, for whom all beauty burns
Like incense in a million urns?
O, beauty, are you not enough?
Why am I crying after love?

— Sara Teasdale

62

TO LUCASTA, ON GOING TO THE WARS

Tell me not, Sweet, I am unkind,
That from the nunnery
Of thy chaste breast and quiet mind
To war and arms I fly.

True, a new mistress now I chase,
The first foe in the field;
And with a stronger faith embrace
A sword, a horse, a shield.

Yet this inconstancy is such
As thou too shalt adore;
I could not love thee, Dear, so much,
Loved I not Honor more.

— Richard Lovelace

LOVE IS ENOUGH

Love is enough: though the World be a-waning,
And the woods have no voice but the voice of complaining,
  Though the skies be too dark for dim eyes to discover
The gold-cups and daisies fair blooming thereunder,
Though the hills be held shadows, and the sea a dark wonder,
  And this day draw a veil over all deeds pass'd over,
Yet their hands shall not tremble, their feet shall not falter:
The void shall not weary, the fear shall not alter
  These lips and these eyes of the loved and the lover.

—William Morris

SHE WAS A PHANTOM OF DELIGHT

She was a phantom of delight
When first she gleamed upon my sight;
A lovely apparition, sent
To be a moment's ornament;
Her eyes as stars of twilight fair;
Like twilight's, too, her dusky hair;
But all things else about her drawn;
A dancing shape, an image gay,
To haunt, to startle, and waylay.

I saw her upon nearer view,
A spirit, yet a woman too!
Her household motions light and free,
And steps of virgin-liberty;
A countenance in which did meet
Sweet records, promises as sweet;
A creature not too bright or good
For human nature's daily food;
For transient sorrows, simple wiles,
Praise, blame, love, kisses, tears, and smiles.

And now I see with eye serene
The very pulse of the machine;
A being breathing thoughtful breath,
A traveller between life and death;

The reason firm, the temperate will,
Endurance, foresight, strength, and skill;
A perfect woman, nobly planned,
To warm, to comfort, and command;
And yet a spirit still, and bright
With something of angelic light.

—*William Wordsworth*

67

INDEX

Set in Linofilm Palatino,
a 20th-century typeface resembling a Venetian,
designed by Hermann Zapf of Frankfurt.
Printed on Hallmark Crown Royale Book paper.